# DOWNTIME

Published by Gunpowder Press
David Starkey, Editor
PO Box 60035
Santa Barbara, CA 93160-0035

Cover Photo: James Hoey

ISBN-13: 978-1-957062-05-1

www.gunpowderpress.com

# Downtime

## Poems from the Couch

### Gary Soto

Gunpowder Press • Santa Barbara
2023

## ACKNOWLEDGMENTS

Some of these poems have appeared in *American Journal of Poetry*, *Cloudbank*, *Huizache*, *I-70*, *Interlitq*, *New American Writing*, *Pedestal*, *Salt*, *San Pedro River Review*, and *Valparaiso Literary Review*.

The poet wishes to thank Christopher Buckley and Carolyn Soto for their help in shaping the collection. Further gratitude goes out to David Starkey and Chryss Yost—they're making literature happen.

To Ron McFarland
A scholar who knows

# Contents

## Travel Plans

Won't get to Peru. Bolivia is out of the question.
Siberia? I wouldn't live to tell the grandkids
Of the sand that creeps along the steppes.
Can't say I'll suck on a hookah in Cairo
Or sample grasshoppers in Chiapas.
A toboggan ride in Greenland?
Reindeer meat in Estonia?
I would love to befriend a bunny in the Highlands
And choke down a plate of haggis.
The Taj Mahal is off the radar
As is flyfishing in Mongolia—
Tempting, but no. *Saludos* to Argentina
And Spain, but no to the Azores at twilight,
The sunsets on the water, then not on the water.

I have a grasp on my limitations.
Won't tap a toe to accordion street music in Paris,
Pet a duck in the Cotswolds,
Or retrace my ancestral steps
Up Teotihuacan. Won't bicycle
A country that I can't spell—is it Lechenstein?
Shake the paw of a comrade in Bulgaria? No can do.
Cuba? *Ay, papi*, to ride shotgun in a '55 Chevy,
A convertible of course, my hair loss
More evident when we pick up speed,
The tip of my cigar glowing ruby red.

I'm not much of a traveler,
Though my ambition is to spin
A prayer wheel in Tibet.
And like Philip Larkin, I would love to go to China
If I could get back on the same day.

# Elegy

in memory of Jon Veinberg

What's the legal speed limit for clouds?
From where I stand on a dry front lawn
My guess is twenty-miles-an-hour,
Fifteen near a school crosswalk.
But for you, amigo, the second
Of three friends to die in a drought year,
My guess is the speed of a gondola,
A slow paddling, with dust in your eyelashes,
As you reached the edge of our badass town.

Never knew you to be in a hurry,
Just the puttering sort feeling for your car keys
And pausing on the lawn, looking back at the house,
Thinking, Did I forget to put the cat back in the fridge?—
No, the milk I mean. This was our joke,
Two Fresno poets leaning toward forgetfulness.
I said, "Jon, let's live not only
Until the cat is in the fridge
But also the dog and the bilingual parrot!"

I don't know where you're buried,
Or if sunshine outlines your grave.
But on the headstone inside my head
I chisel, "Loved cheese and bread,
Had kind words for blood sausages."
And so where are you, anyhow?

Friend, I intend to set cheese and bread on a picnic table,
Grill sausage but let the trotters get away.
I'll toss a salad, uncap a bottle of Estonian beer,

Rework the joke about the Greek doctor and the Irish patient,
Slap my knee and say, "That's a good one."

I have more to say to the dead than the living.
I sigh at this truth, finish my beer.
And when I open the fridge
I may find the cat. Forgetful me,
I've aged since you rowed away on a cloud.
If I find the dog and bilingual parrot
Next to the milk and ketchup,
Then—and only then—I may shiver
From the cold mist rolling out the open door.

And the legal speed limit for a cloud?
Not sure. But the face in the cloud, eased along
By wind, belonged to my friend.

## Six Degrees of Separation

I shake hands with the grandson
Of a high school wrestler who pinned me
In thirteen seconds, 1967.

I'm introduced to a teen
Who asks, Is it true you dated my grandma?
She's dead, you know.

The face of a junior high bully
Appears on a homemade tortilla.
Jaime, I ask, how did you do that?

The family cat that was put down in fall
Shows up as a kitten in spring—
The flirty thing prances right into the kitchen.

My wife and I are greeted by flies
At a picnic table—
Cousins to the ones back home?

The landline rings
And a voice asks, Are you that Gary?

My wife's auntie remembered some other auntie
Who was related by adoption
On the Mori side—
She has a photo somewhere.

A happy memory as I step into my pajamas—
Bless you, Billie Rae Tupper,
My darling who spit out her chewing gum
And let me go whole hog.

My mother, gone two years,
Appears in the reflection of a shop window—
Looking, just looking.

When I take a step back
The reflection on the window
Just dies, a separation
That makes me hurry away.

## All Day

What secret did a minor god breathe into my ear?
Buy low on Monday, sell high on Thursday?
Check my zipper before leaving the house?

I sit up from my nap on the couch, look around—
Several books on the two armchairs
In our mid-century living room.

I lay back on the couch,
Hands behind my head.
I consider my splayed feet
(Physical evidence of indecision?)
And watch my belly rise and fall.

I sleep, I wake.
When I sit up again
Coins fall from my pocket.
One coin, I note, is large as a pocket watch,
And Greek, it appears. I have no memory
Of visiting that island country.
Adventurous me.

Then the noise I've been waiting for all day.
I tiptoe down a hallway
To the door that leads to the garage.
I flick on the light. A mouse looks up,
Head caught in a throw-away trap.

I close the door on him—
Sorry, I sigh, very sorry for your trouble.

But where was I?
That's right, the couch.
I return to the living room,
Where several pairs of reading glasses
Track my shuffling steps.
Sunlight pours through the window.
The curtain lifts like a skirt.
I'm 71, confused by the splash of soup
On my white shirt.
My scalp itches for a single idea.

And as for the mouse in the trap?
After my lunch of soup and two crackers,
I'll shovel a small hole and roll him in,
My one success on a very busy day.

## Thinking about Hemingway

Africa in '32, Spain in '36,
France a decade later
And then Cuba,
Where he purchased a boat
Rigged with a single sail, with a motor perhaps,
And learned to tie knots
In the failing light of a picturesque harbor.

Fingers, he was all heavy fingers,
His typing like the pounding
Of elephant footsteps, rough and loud.
He carried in his big river heart all the elephants
He ever shot at close range.

He was a writer with a story to declare.
In his fifties, he stepped into the surf
And roared at the surf.
He launched his boat near the end of his life.
He had duty to snag a fish
That was not a fish
But a metaphor, man and the sea
Light caught on the sea,
The struggle of landing a big one, etc.

Hemingway got me thinking
About the flavor of metaphor
On a clean, white plate.

# Stranger on the Commuter Train

An artist type in dirty jeans
And a sweatshirt that blazes the face
Of Whitney Houston, mid-career,
Totters down the aisle
Of a rolling train,
Hand on every other loopy overhead rope.

He stops, considers my wife,
Sees that the seat next to her is free.
He sits.

From across the aisle
I'm thinking
Well, he likes what he sees,
A well-dressed woman, hair done nicely,
Bracelet, necklace with its own teasing shine,
A clutch purse as soft as a well-behaved kitty.

And I like what I'm seeing,
My wife getting hit on.
I stand, legs wide to keep my balance
Against the train's sudden shift—
It's a gripping drama for me.

He asks my wife, You going to work?
She looks at him, turns the page
Of her magazine she's reading,
Says, No.

The train rushes through a tunnel.

I hear him ask, What kind of work do you do?
My wife ignores him.

The train comes out of the tunnel.

He asks, Guess what I do?
My wife looks at him,
Says, I don't want to have this conversation.

He nods his head,
Pulls at the front of his T-shirt
Until Whitney's face stretches like taffy,
He gets up, hand clutching the rope above him.

The stranger turns and looks at me,
Our eyes red from what we overdid last night.
He's a painter, I'm a poet.
I want to tell him,
She's not talking to me either.

# The Wife's Shoe Closet

When he opens her closet
The husband finds pumps, sandals, heels,
Flats and platforms, *zoris*,
Cowboy boots, clogs and mules,
Shoes for beginning tap, ballet slippers,
Dozens lined up in the closet,
Nearly all from suburban outlets—
Leather and vegan leather,
Cloth-lined, wool-lined,
Vintage, out-of-this-world styles,
Some shaved from cedar,
Some with brass do-dads,
Bitsy buckles, straps and Velcro.
Hecho in India? Yes.
Hecho in Italy? A mighty Yes.
Imports all, it seems,
And a pair of Jimmy Choo ankle boots
Bundled in a cloth bag.

He learns this: Her shoes,
If they hurried out of his life,
Would run all over his resoled, deadbeat loafers.

# Career Change During the Pandemic

I tell my wife that I intend to study medicine.
From her end of the couch
She says, not looking up
From her sewing,
Think of the wounds that will never close.

I sip my wine, sip a second time.

I clear my throat and speak up—
I plan to specialize in pediatrics.
She says, Leave the children to their band aids.

No, cardiology in a spic-and-span room.
She says, That's right, pull the heart out
And replace it with a ham hock.

Immunology has new areas of growth.
She says, OK, spell that word.
She bites her thread, bites a second time.

Picture me as an anesthesiologist.
She says, Think of your patients sleeping
Until Jesus tickles them awake.

Ear and toe specialist at Stanford Medical.
She says, You mean ear and throat—right?

I stall, I reflect.
Isn't it ear and toe,
A top to bottom annual checkup?

I sip my wine—sip, sip.
I take off my reading glasses
And the lenses flash another idea.

I got it, I say,
Psychiatry in a tall phallic skyscraper.
She laughs and says, You can be Dr. Wacko
And the patient at the same time.

A podiatrist with a small office in a strip mall
She says, The patients arrive walking
And crawl away
With their severed toes trying to catch up.

I like my couch,
The halo of lamplight over my shoulder.
I pour myself another glass of wine.
I slap my thigh—I know, liposuction.
I know, she mocks,
How about a male girdle?

I stall. I think,
My wife is not encouraging.
She doesn't even look up
From her handiwork—
Needle goes into the fabric,
Then out of the fabric,
Like surgery, I think.
What is she making anyhow?

I sip, sip again.
Oh, I know, a lab coat

For our doctor daughter.
How sweet!

She looks me up and down,
Hugs herself.
Guess again.
A straightjacket for poets,
One-size fits all.

# Inflation

Artichokes have spiked in price, kale and spuds,
Bags of frozen peas,
Chicken thighs, chickens breasts,
Domestic wines, beer and sparkling water,
Dented cans of tuna that were once 3 for $2.00—
Now, what, three bucks apiece?
The roll of quarters from the bank teller?
The coins did just that, rolled away.
Life is costly, so costly. Things go up, mostly.

On my couch, with a deadly book
On the lives and times of right-wing Vikings,
I glance down at the windless sail of my crotch.
I think, Swashbuckling six incher,
Do what the spuds are doing,
Inflate, stand up, show thyself,
Cast a shadow on the wall,
And be the rumor that the old guy,
A scholar of sorts,
Is keeping up with that pound of hamburger
And closing in on a T-bone steak!

## Sign Painter

A sign painter
(Buddy of a buddy of mine)
Was up on a ladder
When three guys
Shirtless, lean as alligators,
Yelled, Fool, when you come down
We gonna rob you.
You hear us, fool?

One *loco* gripped
And wiggled the ladder,
Let the vibration
Of fear work through
The sign painter's body,
The brush in his hand
Dripping like a snow cone
Tear-shaped drops of blue paint.

Again, it was a buddy
Of a buddy, though I will paint
A picture to fill out
A Fresno scene, midday,
With dogs nosing burger wrappers
And every other *loco*
Kicking around
With pants cut off at the knees,
All in tank tops,
With tattoos inked
To their shiny Day-of-the-Dead skulls.
Gapped-teeth crazies
Breathing death—
That's how I paint them.

The sign painter considered,
The gators down below,
Then followed the flight
Of two ravens,
Black as pallbearers.
He squeezed his eyes shut
And saw what he loved best:
Wife at home, three kids in school,
House and the house's front lawn...

Better not drip blue
On me, *cabron*, one *loco*
Warned—*tu sabes*, know what I mean?
The sign painter
Tossed the brush
Onto the roof
And floated down three twenties,
Followed by a ten for the favor
Of not kicking over
The ladder.
               Blue
And red, Fresno gang colors,
The two colors
Of our waving flag. Add white
As in the white of a T-shirt
And you get America,
Graffiti no six-inch brush
Could ever begin
To paint over.

## Whittling Us Down

After school I saw a kid with holes in his socks,
Big gapers. I passed him on the street
And looked back,
Then looked at my socks,
Also with holes,
With the soles of my shoes
Yapping like tongues.
What were my deaf-and-dumb shoes telling me?

Then I passed a boy
In a white Catholic shirt,
A boy I sort of knew,
A whole row of buttons gone,
Filaments of thread like dental floss.
I noticed red ink marks around his mouth,
As if a mean nun, transparent
As the Holy Communion wafer,
Had corrected his speech by scribbling his mouth.
And why? *Why?*
He couldn't pronounce "transfiguration"
Without messing up.

Jesus, a carpenter, dressed us however He pleased
And sent us out into the world
Against the grain, a student workforce
That jumped over leaf fires in the gutter,
Practice for adulthood, for another kind of hell.

## Dog Years

Clouds have stalled in the eyes
Of an old dog. The purplish tongue drips.
His hind legs are dead,
I guess, because they're up,
Like landing gear, with small wheels
Attached to his hind end.

The dog sniffs the air,
Then rolls toward a leaf
Curled, crisp, hopelessly common.

He stares me down.
The clouds in his eyes chug across the surface
Of his pupils, westward it seems,
A wind carrying them toward blindness.

The dog rolls away,
One wheel squeaking.
I look down at the leaf
And think that I've become like that,
Common and not worth sniffing.

In an hour the sun
Rolls away without the aid of wheels.
Then dinner, then a proper drink on the couch,
Then a few steps down the hallway to bed.
In sleep, my legs kick for traction.

# Tracking

If I attached a library pencil to my shoe,
As sort of a tracker, I would find
That I've been going in a circle—
Or sort of a circle, with roundish markings
Of my day's outing in Fresno's Chinatown,
A ghost town these days. A cat looks up,
Races to greet the rat and the rat's children.
The rivers of broken glass, a buzz from the overhead pole,
A homeless soul counting his fingers...
The beauty of coming home.

My pencil scribbles my message,
The message that a young man can get in a car
And drive away, then return like a comet,
All edges broken off. You get out of your two-seater
And pick up where you left off.
The cat is missing, the childhood dog,
An uncle's banana-colored parrot
That could pry off bottle caps—
Useful talent after a workday.

And just up this alley
Japanese stores, Komoto's and Kiku's Florist...
Figures who walked these streets,
Mr. Kebo and Mrs. Saito, all gone,
The names faded, the overhead lights off
At New China Cafe. In the eaves
Of the Buddhist temple,
Pigeons warble prayers.

The Mexico Café is gone,
The manju shop, Renge's pharmacy,
Dr. Taira, a somber man, retired not long
After the "A" fell from the Aztec Theater's marquee.
Even the tumbleweeds got out of town.

Who replaced the tamale man at C & Tulare?
Who boarded up the Rainbow Ballroom?
Lucy's Flowers? What sweet scent blooms in her place?
Dick's Clothing, the shoe repair shop,
The underground gaming house...tables
Were overturned after the dice spun a last dance.
The Konko Church moved when the freeway came in.
In one generation the Mexican Baptists
Became English speaking.

The pencil on my shoe tracks my circling
Around Chinatown, midday.
I stop at Central Fish—
Udon noodles, lukewarm tea and a fortune cookie,
A slip of paper that says You travel far.
I'm out the door and up an alley.
Minutes later I hover over a small springtime puddle,
A cloud trembling in the reflection.

I held a girl's hand not far from where I stand.
Took a labor bus at that far corner
Where churros sell for two for a dollar.
Rifled through a second-hand store
And found a jacket—a girlfriend
Embroidered Chinese dragons on the shoulders
And for a long winter I was the Mexican Bruce Lee.

I looked up, hand over my brow.
Wise-Ole Grandpa, dead a dozen years...
He was loping like a camel across a vacant lot,
When he stopped, turned and warned me with a skeletal finger,
*Always use a condom and never go home.*

## Seeing Myself as a Stone

Maybe I was the last birth on Braly Street
April 1952, pushed out and brown as a common stone.
In time I was kicked down the street,
Followed by other stones,
Brown hardheaded kids without luster,
Without worth. But bless me,
Bless the other brown stones,
For sometimes we glistened if touched by rain.

Maybe my birth carried with it a parable,
Something about a stone inside a weathered shoe—
No, let's recall the parable regarding stone soup,
Winter, with frost in each nostril,
Teeth chattering like stones,
Eyes of stone, hearts of stone.

I kick this parable down the street.
I was never soup, never much of anything.
I was the stone picked up, turned over,
And tossed absently into the grass.

But this I know of myself:
If hurled in anger, I spoke up
Through the painful howling of others.

## My Relationship with Plants

The two-inch cactus is a sore thumb,
The fertilized lawn the start of a cemetery,
The tulip a cup with an ounce of rain,
The hedge a porous barrier
Against the neighbor's repeated playing
Of The Carpenter's Greatest Hits.

I like my house, I like my garden.
The white wisteria is a local branch of the cosmos,
The dandelions yellow buttons on the gray coat of gravel,
The hybrid rose a target for the honeybee,
The snapdragons sentries near the front door.

With rake and shovel, I'm a sentry in the backyard.
I recognize my chores. I go to my knees
And crawl like a centipede, pulling up weeds.
I sneeze dust, I wince from the sun.

An hour passes, the bees disappear.
Seated on the garden bench I sip my iced tea,
Observe my handiwork, consider
The leaves rustling with ill-fated rumor.
I consider the pear tree the center of attention,
The camellia royalty in wind,
The moss soft padding on a granite rock.
I drink my tea, wipe the corner of my mouth.
The Iceland Poppies are brief as sparklers.
In time, the spider turns clockwise
On a deflated mushroom.
The dead tree stump along the row of cat graves?

A piece of furniture,
A place to sit and think
How the four seasons of my childhood have become two,
Hot and cold. The apples drop in summer,
Not fall. My hand chooses the apple,
But my tongue will make its decision—
The apple sweet as memory.

## A Thursday Like Any Other

The deepest measure of time?
Yesterday's sandwich, which was tuna
I think, with a beefsteak tomato I believe,
And devoured a few minutes before noon.
No, I take that back, something like ten to one,
With a blade of shadow on the wall.

The blade falls, and another day
Is hacked off, bloodless,
The spurt of tomato splashed onto the front
Of my vintage Hawaiian shirt.

This is my sense of time,
Lunch and shadows, the wind at the window,
And a plate displaying a few, nearly visible, crumbs.

# Monday Morning

Under the pressure of a bread knife,
The cantaloupe cracks open—
This is me getting to work.
A pleasurable balance of hot and cold at the kitchen sink—
This is me with my chore,
A wash up of spoon and bowl.
I look up from the sink—
The cat is licking his murderous paw,
He who takes a life, then purrs on the couch.
Only yesterday he cornered our mouse in residence.
What did he leave behind?
The tail like a shoestring,
Four paws that couldn't find traction.

My wife, tiptoeing, searches the pantry—
A bone clicks in her knee, the left one I believe.
Tapping a pencil against a note card,
She's making a list of what she needs
From the store. That's right, she mutters,
We need a can of tomato sauce.

I have no complaint.
I'm not like that luckless mouse.
I swing open the pantry's double doors
And look for myself—
Yes, we could do with a can of tomato sauce,
Maybe a bottle of fat-waisted Mrs. Butterworth,
Certainly long-grain rice to pour into a pot.

Then I turn and become alert as our cat:
A hummingbird outside the kitchen window,
Morning's first performance of everlasting beauty.

## The River

I took a paper sack
Of misused subjunctives
Down to the river
And heaved these infractions,
Each heavy as anchors,
Into the swift current.
I added run-on sentences,
Then sank the tragedy
Of the double negative,
The comma splice,
The jerky stops
Of the semi-colon,
The cagey brackets,
And my dependence
On the exclamation mark!!!!
My idea of poetry?
A 1970s glam rocker
Rhyming "cosmic"
With "duck."
That was close enough.

The river had become
Filthy with high school tears.
Upstream, a waterfall
Reshaped boulders
And enlarged the trout
That lollygagged
Under slimy rocks.
I went in search
Of the young man
I once was, my hair

Black as a raven,
A tribe of hairs
On my chest,
My penis a totem
That held mild touristy interest
In Western Canada.

I went forth in moccasins.
My breath was a rainless cloud
In the cold air.
At a bend in the river
I was greeted by mossy boulders,
Trees, boat-shaped leaves on the surface...
Is this haiku land?
A monk appeared
From the mist,
A rope in his hand,
His small horse no longer
Laden with literary prizes.
He read my fortune cookie,
Said, Brown One, you burned
Your bridges three times,
But you'll appear
In a poetry magazine
From the Midwest,
Circulation of 300 copies.
The monk uncurled his palm,
Showed me pencil shavings,
Broken lead, the rubbings
Of a pink eraser.
He said, Rebuild the pencil
And try it again.

Three times? I burned
My bridges three times?
I thought it was four.
I shrugged and followed this river,
Adding my own human tears
To that body of water.
I was like Pat Boone—
No, I mean Daniel Boone,
Pioneer who trekked
One river after another,
But who was never,
Ever like me, with language
Of mixed metaphors,
As when the stars
Are like lightbulbs
Against the Santa Claus sweater
Of my late Aunt Martha.
That was pretty good,
Close enough.

## Talking about the Afterlife

And I said,
I'm taking flying lessons—
You're gonna be my first passenger.

My poet friend said,
Man, I would have a better chance
With a chimp at the controls.

Laughter without drinks,
Laughter with a sober tear in our eyes.

I said, Oh, the chimp's coming along.
He's the co-pilot.

Then we drank,
And talked about the chance
Of life after this life,
At any altitude,
With or without a grinning chimp.

We tapped beers,
Drank, revisited the saga
Of our hair lost on Highway 99.

Pondered old age and adult diapers.
On the propeller job
Altitude five thousand feet and rising...
You never know how long the flight will last.

## An Afternoon Tete-á-Tete

Shifting for comfort in my mohair recliner,
Friend K studies his beer,
The first of many on a common afternoon.
He tells me that he has answers—yes, answers to how get rid
Of human soot. He wants to set his personal enemies,
Along with people he sort of knows,
Plus internet celebs, academic colleagues, politician...
Set them like tin soldiers
On the rooftop of a hotel fire.

Can you see what I mean, Soto? he scolds
Yes, I can see, I tell the old prof.
Mighty tongues of the hot stuff bursting windows,
The dart-like glass targeting
The lackeys below. The screams
Go beyond city limits. The firefighters
Can't locate the spigot and every other rung
On their ladders is broken. The circling helicopters
Have better things to do.

Earlier, before K's tirade, I shared with him
Text images of my tomato crop,
Enlarging the cherry tomatoes
Until they were like beefsteaks,
Huge suckers with juice that rolls over your knuckles
When you bit into them.
I return to the subject of tomatoes.
I ask, You want to try one?
Picked a few glorious ones this morning.

He ignores my question.
Tomatoes are not on the menu for discussion.
His eyes spark, smoke seeps from his left nostril.
He's mad because the college has given him tenure.
Now he's forced to stay there.

Friend K lights a cigar, continues...
The hotel fire will start in the kitchen,
Appear with a roller bag in the lobby,
Visit the reception desk for check-in,
Lumber down a dark hallway,
And quickly climb floor after floor,
With his enemies, these national leaders and TV hosts,
The luckless adulterer bending over at the ice machine,
All full of human panic. The elevators fail.
The stairway fills with smoke.
The overhead sprinklers trickle like eye drops.

They climb the stairs, these people he loathes.
Smoke stings their puny eyes.
Flames lick their legs hairless.
Sheetrock falls like books onto their heads.
These humans soon find themselves
On the rooftop, where they cough, go to their knees,
Get up from their knees,
Wave their arms and shout to the sky,
Help! Help! I'll be good!

When I laugh, he narrows an eye at me,
Says, This is not funny, Soto—
Nothing funny about the dean
Of Arts and Letters swatting flames
From his toupee. Oh, no, not a chuckling moment.

I ask, Am I one of them?
He thinks for a second, thinks the way
A state college professor thinks
When he's seated in front of the ombudsman.
He says, No, Soto, you escape like you always escape,
Like when the bill comes at the restaurant.

I laugh, tell him he's sitting in my mohair chair
And drinking my beer—be nice.
He pastes the beer bottle label
Onto his sweater—an award for fast thinking?
Literary merit? Employee of the week at a car rental?

Let me guess, I say, they all burn up on the rooftop?
I want to hurry this along
And return to my tomatoes,
A platoon of canned goods in the pantry.

He drinks his drink, wipes his mouth,
Taps ash into a teacup, and answers,
No, some will decide to jump.

## War Games

Three green plastic army men,
Circa the mid-60s, neck deep in the canal's mud,
Rescued while I was volunteering
At a shoreline cleanup.

One soldier was kneeling with a bazooka on his shoulder.
The other two were aiming their rifles,
Ready to exchange fire.
The three were facing the canal
From where the enemy,
Speaking gobbledygook, would approach.
But which evil enemy?
North Korean, North Vietnamese,
Panamanian, Iraqi, Libyan, Iranian, Cuban,
Grenadian, Afghani...
Who's next, the angry bear of Russia?

I pulled these soldiers from the mud,
Wiped their faces with a thumb,
And turned them over—
The bottoms were stamped Made in Japan.
I remembered my own army men,
How I lined them up for battle.
I flicked over every other G. I.
The enemy, I realized, would kill some of us
Before we mowed their whole country down.

Plastic is forever.
War, it appears, is also forever.
The plastic soldiers exhumed from mud?
Body-bagged with the litter.

## Talking Crazy Shit

Gonna bite a tree and spit out a literary masterpiece.
Drink the surf that splashes over my feet—
Man, that's a salty brew.
Iron out the wrinkles of unprofitable raisins.
Repaper a kite and fly it over Ben Franklin's grave.

(I'm applying for a grant
And a friend, winner the previous year,
Said that I should talk crazy shit.)

I chew a fingernail, think deeply, then write...
Once I negotiated an apple from the squirrel's tiny paws.
Witnessed a fish surface from a placid lake and utter, Rosebud.
Rode a donkey to the finish line, with Jesus a close second.
Patted my lap for the bulldog to sit—
The beast stank of a dozen wet wool coats.

(This grant is due by noon,
Pacific Standard Time—twelve minutes to go.)

Yes, I will spend my grant money wisely.
Yes, I appreciate that most people pay taxes.
Yes, in the case of an untimely death on the couch
My grant money will be returned.
No, I will not visit porn sites.
No, I will not visit Cuba, North Korea, or Putin's Russia.

(More time is drained from my life
When I'm forced to Google the capital of North Korea.)

My hero? The astronaut who bounced around on the moon.
No, wait a minute, Marie Curie.
No, not her either... uh, what is Sojourner Truth?

(I get my application in
With thirty seconds to spare—
The capital of North Korea is Pyongyang.)

I stand up, stretch, look down at my waist,
A poet suddenly fascinated by the workings of his belt:
Sometimes I use the third hole,
Sometimes the fourth hole.

Damn, I think,
I forgot to mention my belt,
The poet's liposuction called Hunger.

Let's be honest!
My application was part lie.
My hero is the astronaut.
How he could hold his piss from
When he went up until he came back down!

## Not a Pretty Picture

Drove through the Cotswolds,
A postcard picture of villages,
Thatched roofs, stone fences,
Pubs and mowed pastures,
Hay piles and a gaggle of geese drinking from puddles...
I stopped, stretched my arms skyward,
O, the gratitude to beam like the sun!

I found the two mares nibbling grass,
Their tails swishing about.
                              I know a little history,
Heard about how horses
Once dead
Were stripped
Of their fur and dissolved into glue,
Stirred like oatmeal mush in great vats,
An industry that stopped just after WW II.

I brought an apple to my face,
Ate until the sweetness became tart,
And let my eyes rove
Over the pastoral landscape,
Then once again considered the two mares,
Swaybacked, gray around their muzzles,
Their nostrils moist and dripping.
Am I like them, I thought,
With my remaining days in the pasture?

Two generations earlier,
The old mares would have been the glue
On a lovely postcard stamp.

## Office Work

I found parking in the world,
Walked up concrete steps
That would outlast this and every other job,
And stapled documents together.
I sent out packets—
A clerk in a bordering state
Undid the staples,
Maybe poked his finger on one
And bled on the job.

I answered phones, rifled through files,
And spoke up when I saw "received"
Was spelled "ie" in a gibberish letter
To a Midwest distributor of Bic Lighters.

I was liked, mostly.
I fed our one goldfish
And watered the geranium
Set on the windowsill,
A potted plant that was either pushed
Or jumped, for one morning
It was found on the sidewalk below,
Broken like Humpty Dumpty.

The drama of the electric pencil sharper,
The oven toaster that was a crematorium for our bagels!
The wall calendar yellowed like teeth
And our supervisor toyed with his wart.
This job was a yawner, dull as my white shirt.
The women picked up their purses and left

When I was asked to shred documents,
An illegal act, something about unpaid corporate taxes.

A wisenheimer in our office
Dropped his pants
And sat on the copy machine—
This went out in the afternoon mailing.
A week later I opened a large envelope
And on the first page
Male buttocks as ugly as they come.
And was that part of a sloppily circumcised dick
I was looking at?

I was a weekend Christian at the time,
And thought of Our Lord on the cross,
Nails in his nearly naked body.
Now this, this shameful exposure
Was sent priority mail, at the start of the week—
Shame-shame.

I made my way over to the paper shredder—
The image of the buttocks and dick was ground like pork.

We office workers?
With every poke from a staple,
We cried, Jesus!
And sucked the fuck-you finger like candy.

# Tree Hugger

She comes now and then
To the edge of our yard,
This tree hugger,
Who wraps her arms
Around a giant redwood
Planted in 1952, they say,
The year of my birth, I know,
This seed, this sapling,
This cool length
Of shade in summer.

She hugs the tree,
Bows to it,
Presses a palm to the rough bark.
Sometimes she weeps,
Then walks away,
Her leafy shadow sweeping the sidewalk.

*Silly, I think, silly.*

And this Sunday,
Holy day for many,
I watched her
From my kitchen window,
A wooden spatula in my hand,
Oatmeal in my bowl,
The cat rubbing
Against my leg.
A hug? Is this what
The cat required? She rose up

On her hind legs
And gave my thigh a hug.

*Silly, I think, silly.*

One pagan Monday
This woman hugged the tree
On the edge of our yard.
I put down the spatula
And looked at my bowl
Of oatmeal on the kitchen counter.
My shoulders sunk slightly
When I thought, Who loves me?
The ankle biter called Cat.

The roots of water
That rushed to my eyes.

# Thai Massage in a Strip Mall that Will Go Unnamed

Will it tickle? I asked,
And the stern-faced masseuse seated in a chair,
Rubbing lotion on her wide feet,
Said, No.

That was our conversation.
I lay, shirtless and face down, on the table.
I lowered my head into the paper-lined face cradle,
Looked at the linoleum floor,
With random starburst prints,
And began a conversation
With myself, an out-of-the-blue episode
Of inner regrets.
                              I recalled Hilda Nelson,
The two of us in ninth grade English.
She was beautiful, she was tall,
And she knew more words than me.
She spoke French, some Spanish,
And grasped the physics of blowing a bubble
From her pinkish chewing gum.
Did she like me that fall day in 1965?
Was she waiting for me to take her hand
And ask her, in a tender moment
And behind the privacy
Of a small thirsty hedge,
Ask whether she would
Like me to undo the top buttons
Of her blouse and take a peek,
A righteous sniff maybe?
Or go whole hog and lick
One of her breasts like a candy wrapper?

Now I was 71, with not much to do,
Except to get in my clunker
And drive to a suburban massage parlor,
The front window lined with blinking lights.
I entered, said, Hello, hello,
With the music of two bells on the doorhandle
Overriding my hesitant footsteps.
I was suddenly worried—
Did I leave the iron on back home?

The conversation inside my head sputtered.
The masseuse leapt onto my back,
Gripped the overhead contraption
Of ropes and started walking slowly
As if approaching a level-entry job she dreaded,
And then trod speedily,
As if she was leaving that job
For something better,
With health benefits even.

I laughed a little, then laughed a lot.
The masseuse was wrong—
The massage did tickle, her marching steps
Suddenly military in nature,
Then a clumsy tap-dancing routine
Followed up with the back-and-forth plodding paces
Of a wolverine in a regional zoo.
I laughed and hollered with pleasure
With my head in that cradle thing-y,
Tears springing from my eyes
And bursting on the linoleum floor,
Tears that were like those starburst prints—
Fossilized sobbing of previous geezers?

The masseuse did the Mashed Potatoes
On my back, the Cha-Cha-Cha,
The Locomotion, the Pony and the Twist,
All the dance steps from the 1960s.
I laughed that my life
Was nearly over (thank God),
That not much happened between sunup and sundown,
No wisdom, no encounter with truth or beauty,
Until I arrived at this strip mall,
Fifty-five years later.
This I learned, this only, at a reasonable price.
Through pain and laughter,
With a Thai woman marching on my back,
I realized Hilda Nelson
Hated my guts.

## The Snob

I sample the morsels
From the platter that goes by,
Drink what's offered,
Smile, chitchat,
Show a young lawyer my neck
Bruised from a pushing match on the tennis court.

This is a gathering for a nonprofit,
With dozens in a room
All nibbling, all talking.
The one in heels tall as barstools
Is tipsy and slurring a story
How she once heard bicycles in the sky,
Looked up and said, "No, they were geese."
HAHAHA.

I approach the auction table.
Bid, it shouts, bid for a cause:
A single bottle of red, $100.00.
A basket of cheeses, $50.00.
A pair of tickets to the San Francisco Ballet, $280
A night at a Napa B & B, $460.
I put my name down for cheese.
I promise myself to check in twenty minutes—
No one dare leapfrog my cowardly bid of $7.00.

Then a couple arrives,
A king and queen by their entrance,
Their eyes working from left to right,
And then they see me,

Approach me, the woman glaring
At the glass of wine offered from a platter.
She shoos it away and turns her eyes
To my hanging jowls, she of the taller order,
She of the second marriage to a plastic surgeon,
She of the scowl no doctor can realign,
She of the bitter pennies.
She asks, Is anyone important here?

Only you, I say, only you...
Then check on my cheese.

# The First Day with a Hearing Aid

The dog spoke for me,
A single bark that echoed how I felt
On a day when I learned
That the milk's expiration date had come
And gone, like a holiday. Then in walked
The cat. The cat spoke through me,
A double meow. I petted
Its head and like a trolley conductor
Rang the bell on his collar.

Domestic pets are having their way.
I splashed generous waves
Of the expired milk into the cat's bowl,
Nudged it with a toe into the sunlight
From the kitchen window—
Nature's microwave oven.

The jay outside the window spoke up,
A scolding screech that went
Through me like an electrical shock. Never liked
That sort of bird. I kicked open the kitchen
Door and thought, Go head, birdbrain,
Hop inside. I pictured the jay,
On springy twigs, circling that bowl of milk
And the cat, his fangs the finest cutlery
In nature, suddenly bouncing
On him. And the dog?
The dog would bark
And lap the bowl of milk,
While I, high up on the domestic ladder,

Would lean against the kitchen sink.
I wouldn't be above howling.

The first day with a hearing aid—
The sounds of a lovely slaughter
Right at my feet.

# Composition

Beginning, middle and end,
The rules of composition,
As in the five-paragraph essay that starts,
He was born in a unique time
And ends, He died in a unique time.

I have a little more to say about college essays.
We're all born, we all die,
And the unique part
I'm not so sure. But the middle
Of an essay, as in the middle of life,
Should be longish,
No, downright fat with imported beers,
Platters of oysters and cured meats,
Friendships, clothes,
Dental work, Pilates classes,
Bank deposits, bank withdrawals,
Two or three late model clunkers,
A ramble in an English countryside,
Break ups that sting for a month,
Danceable Motown music, lost keys,
Two credit cards
In case one doesn't work,
The occasional job, love for all.
Pad the essay, make it long,
Namedrop important
And unimportant historical heroes,
Starting with Adam,
Rabble rouser in a fig leaf.
Hell, why not, let's return

To our days of college poverty,
With our pockets turned inside out,
The day-old pizza we called breakfast.
Let's consider our youth,
The consensual doggie-style fucking
With sunshine beaming
Through a dorm window
Onto our glorious asses...
For, really, who wants to come
To the conclusion
Of our five-paragraph lives?

The Kittens

At a local museum,
I'm the volunteer gardener,
The man in khaki, with shovel and snips,
A broom that swats the sidewalk,
The lasso of a long, pliable garden hose
That I drag from the west side
Of the museum to the east side.
The travel time? Five minutes,
Seven if I stop to talk to an onlooker
Just beyond the gate—
Someone's always in need
Of directions, help,
A dollar if you could, please.
The neighborhood slants toward rough.

One fall day, a pleading noise
While I was rolling up
The garden hose. I stepped between
The hybrid brother-and-sister rose bushes
And discovered two newborn kittens,
Eyes closed, crawling. The mother
Just beyond the rose bushes, dead—
A dog, it had to be a dog.

I placed the kittens in the pouch
Of my sweatshirt, drove home.
At home, I called our daughter,
A veterinarian. She came
With small bottles of milk.
They drank, they rotated their ears,

A sign of contentment
Our daughter said.

I went about the rest of my day—
Laundry, grocery shopping, a meeting
In the street with a neighbor,
Phone calls, email, leftovers
For dinner—all the while visiting the kittens
In their box, softened with a bed
Of wash clothes. I petted their heads,
Cooed nice words, prayed,
Held them on a knee.
I watched over them the next day,
And the next, watched their ears,
A sign our daughter said.
I watched the rotations slow,
The ears no longer moving circular
But up and down,
As if waving farewell.

Then they died, these little sisters,
These kittens with the start of tiger stripes.
I tucked them into a pair
Of cloth gardening gloves,
Buried them side by side
Under the apple tree.

My own ears didn't rotate
Until the roses bloomed again.

## What I Learned

This was English, this was us with a huge literature book.
Frost was lost in snow, e. e. cummings handicapped from bad typing,
And T. S. Eliot strolled on a beach, pant cuffs rolled up,
Head down and searching for the letters to spell out his Christian name.

Snow, I heard about it. Bad typing? I could do that.
A beach to scrub your eyes clean? Been there once.
And Edgar Lee Masters? His head was a tombstone,
He the mortician thumbing the pages of a telephone book
To call up the dead.

No fun. As I was sixteen, I wanted dance music.
I asked, Mrs. McGuire, why are these people no fun?
She chuckled, brought a pencil
From her beehive hairdo,
And wrote on a pad on her desk,
Gary asks...

We read Frost, a cold man,
Stuff about fences, snow, apples, birch trees—
Then jumped when the bell clanged its iron tongue.
We shoved our way out of the classroom,
Each of us a picket in a long
And poorly built fence,
And huddled in the courtyard to eat potato chips.

Next class up, biology,
A microscope and my view of scantily clad germs,
Each sort of kissing,
Each sort of eating each other out.

I pulled my eye from the microscope,
Sized up Melissa, a girl I sort of liked, eating a donut,
Then returned my eye to the thumb-printed lens
Of the microscope.

From the third row, always the third row for me,
I learned that saliva and sex were separated by a few germs,
And the rhymes of e. e. cummings, Robert Frost,
And Eliot who spat ash every other Wednesday...
You couldn't dance to what they put down on paper.

## Questions Not Asked in Catechism

Who prompted the finch to visit the lawn?
>The cat and the cat's shiniest fang.

Who fed the worm between storms?
>Mother Earth in all her wetness.

Who sent the geese flying south?
>Mother Earth when she was done with the worm.

Who drank from the plate of milk?
>The cat after he finished the devil's long-tailed rat.

Who questioned the angels?
>God did, but He didn't bother to listen.

Who appeared from a leaf fire in the gutter?
>A mystery man who became the Holy Ghost.

Who righted the child after he fell from his bike?
>A stranger, who offered a dollar to make it all right.

Who was that boy?
>Not Jesus or Abraham, not Buddha or Mohamad,
>More a boy who wept with a hand over his eyes.
>His three wounds? All in his heart.

## Everyone's Disappeared

No emails, no letters, no skywriting
From the poetry gods above. I walk down
The street. It seems everyone's disappeared.
No artists, clowns, acrobats,
Librarians, academics, over-educated baristas,
No sports figures, sports fans,
Hustlers, sex workers, union busters, the homeless,
All the people I ever encountered
On the streets until it is just

Me.

I'm standing on a street
Where cars are abandoned.
The UPS trucks idle, their hazard lights blinking.
Bicycles lay on their sides.
Skateboards and scooters—also abandoned.

Do I have rocks in my head?
I take a step, then another step.
Am I in a science fiction movie?
A remake of *The Day the Earth Stood Still*?
Hello, I call thinly. Is anyone here?

I shrug, do more than shrug—
I shiver. I take a step, then another step.
Will I be alone in my eighties?
Will I show up at the second funeral in a month
And tap a knuckle against a casket,
My mariachi friend tucked nicely inside,

Hands on his belly,
His trumpet tucked under an arm?

I consider this death, consider the silence.
I scoot my butt up onto the hood
Of a Mercedes Benz. I close my peepholes.
I see a chicken pecking the turtle's hard shell
And the turtle regurgitating lettuce—
Share and share alike.
I see a chicken standing
On top of the turtle,
And the turtle crawling around a wet stone,
With a batch of lettuce in his ancient chops.

My vision stops when I hear my name—Gary, you're late!
I spot my wife, dressed to the nines,
Coming out of a store clutching three bags.

I cross the street, hug her.
What do you think of my new shoes?
She asks and clicks her heels—
Who is she now, Dorothy?

How much did they cost?
I ask.

She contorts her face with surprise,
Righteously confused.

*Cost?*

Sweetheart, she says,
At our age everything's free,
Even parking.

Plumbers, fry cooks on the morning shift,
The mariachis at the corner of 14<sup>th</sup>
And International, trilingual nannies,
Boy Scouts, Girl Scouts, drinking buddies,
ESL teachers, janitors, car mechanics,
Everyone I ever encountered
On streets until it is just

Me and my everlasting wife.

# Waiting for Spring

*David Ruenzel, 1955-2015*

I climb a hill
And look over the hill
In search of spring. It's late January,
With the sky boulder gray,
The crunch of frost under my boot steps.

I come upon two campers —
No, the homeless bundled in jackets,
Watch caps down to their brows.
Neither is happy, neither looks at me.
Pray for them, Kami Sama,
Pray that beards unravel
And warm their laps.

A great oak is down,
Split in the middle, its meaty insides white.
Still, a squirrel calls it home.
Two crows screech,
Lift heavily when I approach.

I'm gloveless, clueless.
I should be home,
Not on this hill cut in half by shadows.
My buddy was killed here—
A shot to his shoulder, one to his face.
Blood crawled but didn't get far.
By noon the next day
The wind delivered the rumors of his death.

The sky, feathered with thin clouds, is true,
And the frost that grips the grass is also true.
They say that in ten years the grief cracks, thaws,
Runs its own sweet path.
This is year seven.

Spring won't come for another three years.

## A Place to Read

A regional park, the best I can do
On a Saturday when I'm scheduled
To begin Franz Kafka's *The Metamorphosis*,
The story of a despondent who wakes up
As an insect. This will be fun,
Me on a blanket, the shadow
Of a small paperback shading the sun
From my eyes. I'm committed to this novel,
A classic I should have read in college,
About the time I was spitting up blood
Between hard and easy classes.

I roll onto my belly, a small mound of success,
And grimace at the cry of a landlocked seagull.
I quote Kafka: *The meaning of life is that it stops*.

Still, Hawaii is not far from my thoughts.
A young woman shimmies into a grass skirt,
A coconut falls not far from a sea turtle,
A ukulele is lifted into the arms of a very brown auntie.
Only then do the trees begin to sway
And a wave delivers a six-pack of Sapporo.

I correct my thoughts. I want to be with my wife,
Presently on the couch I imagine,
A bundle of yarn in her lap.
If I could only sleep in her lap
And wake to find myself knitted into a colorful Afghan.

The novel falls away, the sun with it.
I nap, hugging my insect-like bones.
Kafka died with his head over a bowl,
And lived up to his word.

## This May Not Be a Poem

My buddy's wife invented a new color
Of anger, locomotive black if you want to know,
With her husband—my buddy—standing on the train tracks.

She circled him around the kitchen table,
Cornered him by the fridge, and asked
With her hand on his collar, Did you fuck Lisa?
My buddy nibbled his mustache,
Breathed in, breathed out,
And whimpered, It wasn't in there that long.

Dead on the tracks

## A Call from Brenda

Got a call about my 50<sup>th</sup> high school reunion—
A picnic by a river, tents for shade,
A banner to sign, steaks if you're up to paying thirty dollars,
Chicken for twenty, Polish dogs for ten.
The bean dip is free.

I asked, Who's this again?
Brenda, a voice said. I live in Tulare, you silly.
She asked, You know any classmates who have died?

(I didn't know them when they were living—
Dead, I wouldn't begin to recognize them.)

Brenda, I couldn't remember
And thought, Well, hell, we're not getting any younger.
I moved my landline phone from one ear
To the next and said, Put me down for chicken.

Then she talked and talked—
A fertile family with eleven grandchildren,
Three out of college, two in prison, the others with jobs.
I butted in, Yeah, I read
About one of our classmates dying—John.

Oh, that's horrible, she moaned,
Then asked, Which John? Avakian or Garcia?

*Saint Peter who works the conveyor belt,*
*Who leads us to our eternal peace,*
*How do I answer this?*

I closed my eyes, opened them.
I said, The John who would have chosen steak.

# Hobo, 1957

Mrs. Oda opened the screen door
To a hobo in a coat that was never new to him,
Shoes that once belonged to another,
A beard still climbing out of his face.
Do you have some eats?
That was his question and the largest question
He would ask that summer day.

The screen door closed,
The tractor in the field pulled at weeds,
And the chickens pecked gems
From the morning scattering of seed.
Five minutes later Mrs. Oda reappeared,
Offering lunch on a paper plate.

Thank you were his words,
Thank you, thank you
From a mouth somewhere hidden in his beard.

A sandwich cut in half, a pickle in wax paper,
Figs and Graham crackers, a glass of water
With ice cubes bumping into each other
As he walked to sit in the shade
Of a walnut tree. There,
He shooed away a muscular fly—
This was his meal,
One o'clock in the afternoon,
For the postman had come and gone.

Hunger, let's note, has no clock to wind.
For a such a man,
The alarm is always ringing.

## Not Good News

I have more dead friends
Than living ones. I wish I could shake salt
On that cold truth and eat my words.
But I'm sincere. Now, let's see,
Among the dead there's...
And among the living there's...

I could invite both parties
To a candlelight gathering,
A three-course meal—
Cloth napkins from the drawer,
Soup spoons for a hearty chowder,
A basket of bread and butter,
Cheese shaved from a wheel,
And a Riesling from landlocked Austria.
The conversation? Something neutral—
The soil erosion along the Mississippi Delta?

The dead will sit on one side,
The living on the other. Elbows off
The table, napkins on our laps.
Let's start slowly, then speed up
The conversation, empty the bottle
And bring another from the fridge.

At the end of the evening,
I may discover that I have more to say
To the dead than the living.

# What You Can't Do

Pull Fidel's beard,
Bicycle the Himalayas,
Strike up a conversation with a bowl of oatmeal,
Reclaim my hair from a comb,
Reconnect the radiator hose of my sex life,
Give a pint of blood to refresh an anemic chimp,
And accept on behalf of an actor in rehab
A daytime Emmy.

I tap a pencil against my thigh—
Oh, that's right, I can't shake hands
With a starfish, rumble with a bear,
Judge the value of bitcoins,
Reupholster my buttocks in genuine leather,
Or build an aircraft carrier
Applying the geometry of a bent paperclip.

We have our limits.
I tried singing, I tried sports,
I tried Ikebana flower arranging.
I once mounted a horse
And from that height stared down a rattler—
A yarn for three chords of cowboy poetry.

Two wives? Out of the question.
Three friends? Let's call on Curly, Larry and Moe.
A barroom brawl? Amigo,
Fighting flies circling your shot glass
Is harder than you think.
And to think that when I met Fidel
I was inches away from pulling his beard.

Imagine my blood on a prison wall.

# Sunday Morning After a Saturday Night

To eat around the wormy hole
Of an apple, on a Sunday mind you,
Brain addled from tumbler after tumbler of proper drink—
What was it last night, cognac? Vermouth? Grog from Siberia?

I pull the apple away from my unshaven face,
Note the hole, a tunnel of dark that could whistle in wind.
Where did the worm go? Did it fly off
As a butterfly? That's what they do, right?

And as I'm addled, as I'm suddenly a Catholic repentant
On a Sunday morning, the sky blue
And tinted with hope, etc. etc., I think of Eve dressed
In translucent fig leaves—boy, she's a hottie.

Eve bats her eyes at Adam, then presents the apple,
Which is not Fuji or Golden Delicious,
Not Gala or McIntosh or Granny Smith,
Or a cheap-ass, plastic bag from Grocery Outlet.

No, this apple is the first of the very first.
Adam bites into the apple. The apple juice
Drips from his chops—no like, no like at all!
He has tasted worm, he has swallowed deceit, etc., etc.

What is man's squirming tongue but a worm,
Worm that offers lies and half-truths, some lashing
Of the lower congress of both men and women.
What is the human brain but the noodles of an extinct warthog.

It's a thirsty Sunday morning. I'm not in church,
I'm not anywhere. The picture window offers a blue sky
And some clouds, I see, all passing, all with hope,
All with tumbler after tumbler of clear lovely water.

I could drink to that.

# Memory and the Beauty of Blueberries

Is this old age? The faucet drips,
The linoleum blisters when you walk on it.
The magnets on the refrigerator crawl down
With the gravity of expired coupons and doctor bills.
Sometimes I roll my tongue in my mouth.
Is this thirst or desire? Is this pain
Or my foot going to sleep? I know the factory
Inside my stomach has gone quiet.
My hair falls as I stand.
The smirk on my face?
I relinquish it, pass it on to the duck
That's more decoy than living feathers.

They say that blueberries improve memory.
If so, back up the truck, unload this fruit by the pallet.
Let me swallow this potent berry
That's mostly ink, a squirt on the tongue,
A stain on the corners of the mouth,
A marble of thought held between thumb
And index finger, a miracle pill if you like.

Blueberries in my morning cereal!
Now where's my fork.

# The Visiting Poet

My poet friend sits in my mohair chair.
He has something to tell me
After the air clears of cigar smoke.

Finally, he sits up, makes his report.
Listen up, Soto, here's how it is.
With eyes closed he recites,

*Poetry will stop a mugger dead in his tracks,*
*Make him skip backwards*
*As he holds up his pants with one hand*
*And salutes with the other—*
*Sorry, prof, sorry.*

So says my friend in less elegant words,
His cigar tip burning red as a sore.

I regard his input, rewet my lips
With a sip of so-so scotch.
Is this urban myth? I inquire,
You mean, like, poetry stops crime?

The red of his cigar deepens
When he inhales—Yes, poetry stops crime.
The smoke lifts toward the ceiling.

An idea comes to me.
I ask my friend in the endowed chair
Of afternoon bullshit,
Yeah, but what kind of poetry?

He closes his eyes,
Opens them in a slow rebirth of thought.
He perfumes the air with the smoke
Of a so-so cigar.

Sonnets usually. Rhymed couplets for sure.

# Roadkill

The squirrel has lost its charm,
Mouth open, one claw up in the sky,
Blood like a bib, tail still moving
In the breeze of afternoon traffic. Its eyes hold
A patch of reddish sky,
Its tongue a taste of autumn air.
What was it doing but crossing the road,
For it, too, had to eat. Just out of its reach,
An acorn for winter, sustenance
For wherever springtime squirrels go—
A tunnel of spiraling ivy, the crack of twigs,
Under the boards of a toppled fence.

I look up and around—
The traffic is faster than I remember.
The speeding headlights will find us all.

## Waistband

Can't decide whether to live
With a thirty inch or thirty-two-inch waist—
Then the sudden memory
Of me jumping over a rose bush,
1963, my waist then eighteen inches,
My ambition the holly bush by the front window,
With mom looking out, stepfather looking on,
Both thinking, He's going to jump over the house—
You'll see, neighbors!

Fuck it! At 71 I fork a third sausage,
Scoot potatoes onto a plate, pound the bottom
Of a nearly depleted ketchup bottle,
Add translucent onions done with their crying,
Salt and pepper, chili flakes,
A sprinkle of Tabasco sauce to quicken my steps.
I gaze up from my plate—
Hunger is the foremost temptation.
How I would love to strangle the neighbor's hen
And roast it lickety-split.

Fork in hand, I look down at my cat—
Milk on his whiskers, amber light in his lean eyes.
I smile at this little fellow.
How did he learn to open the fridge
But by observing.

# A Pony Called Beauty

Outside London, at Osterley's grand parkland,
We strolled with our shadows in front of us,
Then behind us as we turned east—
A pony was standing behind a fence.
I petted her nose and moved her mane out of her eyes.
I saw myself on the surface of her eyes,
Then saw my wife standing behind me,
A red brooch on her collar.

This was 2011.
Wars followed, famine, presidential lies,
Bodies pitched by the hundreds into Gulf Stream.
Fires climbed trees, earthquakes rattled our bones,
Covid-19 shook hands with my neighbors,
Every sort of menace the world brings to beauty.

Ten years later...
We returned to London, to this grand parkland,
And this is true as blue is true,
The grass and the wind are true.
We followed the same road, wet from a cloudburst,
And stopped before the fence—
My heart, my wife's heart, trotted two beats.
The same pony came up to us,
Now shorter, muddied
From the terror of standing in rain.
Beauty, I nearly cried, you've waited.

I pulled the mane from her forehead.
Once again my wife and I lived briefly,
So perfectly fit, on the surface of her eyes.

# I Picture It

My dear wife walks across a vacant lot
Where it's always 1952,
With a blimp in the eastern sky,
Factory noise down the street,
Trucks like hell-bent rhinos,
A single plum tree that flowers in all seasons.

My wife pulls a Ziplock bag
From her purse, opens it,
Looks in, says, Goodbye, Gary, it was pretty fun...
And pours my ashes
Onto the sandy ground
Where I once played, fought,
And made shards of broken bottles
Wink with sunlight—my childhood fun.

She shakes out my remains,
Says a Shinto prayer with eyes mostly closed.
She next glances up at the inverted bowl of polluted sky:
A cigar-shaped blimp, the shreds of clouds.
She turns to the rustle from the knee-high weeds.
Boots, my cat? Has he come to show me the way?

How the sand sucks up tears,
And there are tears.
She prays a Christian prayer just to be sure,
Then shakes the Ziplock bag,
The remaining inch or two
Of human ash directionless in wind,
Faint as a shadow, the stuff of rumor that became fact:
My human soot that didn't fly very far.

# About the Poet

Gary Soto, born and raised in Fresno, California, is the author of thirteen poetry collections for adults, most notably *New and Selected Poems*, a 1995 finalist for both the Los Angeles Times Award and the National Book Award. His prose titles include *Living Up the Street, A Summer Life, Jesse, Buried Onions,* and *The Effects of Knut Hamsun on a Fresno Boy*. He has written for the stage, including the libretto *Nerdlandia*, the musical *In and Out of Shadows*, and the one-act *The Afterlife*. He is the author of "Oranges," the most anthologized poem in contemporary literature. He lives in Berkeley, California.

*Other titles in the*

GUNPOWDER PRESS
CALIFORNIA POETS SERIES

଼

*Gatherer's Alphabet*
Susan Kelly-DeWitt

଼

*Our Music*
Dennis Schmitz

଼

*Speech Crush*
Sandra McPherson

# More from Gunpowder Press

*Mother Lode* - Peg Quinn
*Raft of Days* - Catherine Abbey Hodges
*Unfinished City* - Nan Cohen
*Original Face* - Jim Peterson
*Shaping Water* - Barry Spacks
*The Tarnation of Faust* - David Case
*Mouth & Fruit* - Chryss Yost

## BARRY SPACKS POETRY PRIZE

*Accidental Garden* - Catherine Esposito Prescott
*Like All Light* -Todd Copeland
*Curriculum* - Meghan Dunn
*Drinking with O'Hara* - Glenn Freeman
*The Ghosts of Lost Animals* - Michelle Bonczek Evory
*Posthumous Noon* - Aaron Baker
*Burning Down Disneyland* - Kurt Olsson
*Instead of Sadness* - Catherine Abbey Hodges

## ALTA CALIFORNIA CHAPBOOKS

*On Display* - Gabriel Ibarra
*Sor Juana* - Florencia Milito
*Levitations* - Nicholas Reiner
*Grief Logic* - Crystal AC Salas

## SHORELINE VOICES PROJECT

*Big Enough for Words: Poems and Vintage Photographs
from California's Central Coast*
David Starkey, George Yatchisin, and Chryss Yost editors
*While You Wait: A Collection by Santa Barbara County Poets*
Laure-Anne Bosselaar, editor
*To Give Life a Shape: Poems Inspired by the Santa Barbara Museum of Art*
David Starkey and Chryss Yost, editors
*What Breathes Us: Santa Barbara Poets Laureate, 2005-2015*
David Starkey, editor
*Rare Feathers: Poems on Birds & Art*
Nancy Gifford, Chryss Yost, and George Yatchisin, editors
*Buzz: Poets Respond to SWARM* - Nancy Gifford and Chryss Yost, editors